THE DOVE DOVE

HEE
HEE
HO HO
HA HA

THE DOVE DOVE

FUNNY HOMOGRAPH RIDDLES

by MARVIN TERBAN

illustrated by
TOM HUFFMAN

CLARION BOOKS
TICKNOR & FIELDS: A HOUGHTON MIFFLIN COMPANY
NEW YORK

Clarion Books
Ticknor & Fields, a Houghton Mifflin Company

Printed in the U.S.A.

P 10 9 8 7 6 5 4 3 2

Library of Congress Cataloging-in-Publication Data

Terban, Marvin.
The dove dove

Summary: A collection of over seventy riddles using homographs, words that are spelled the same but differ in meaning and pronunciation.
1. Riddles, Juvenile. 2. Homonyms—Juvenile humor.
[1. Riddles. 2. English language—Homonyms]
I. Huffman, Tom, ill. II. Title.
PN6371.5.T42 1988 818'.5402 88-2611
ISBN 0-89919-723-X

PA ISBN 0-89919-810-4

To my dear sisters, Loraine Freedman and Roslyn Penn,
who don't look alike and don't sound alike

—M.T.

To Adam J.

—T.H.

Contents

DOVE

What Are Homographs?

English is a very puzzling language. It's filled with many confusing words, and none are trickier than homographs.

The homographs in this book are words that are spelled exactly alike, but they are pronounced differently and they have different meanings.

Sometimes homographs

change their vowel sounds (chapter 1),
change the sound of the letter s (chapter 2),
shift accents from one syllable to another (chapter 3),
or add extra syllables (chapter 4).

Some homographs are related in meaning, like

the verb **inSULT** (to make an impolite remark) and the noun **INsult** (an impolite remark).

Sometimes the words are not related at all, such as

dove (a bird associated with peace) and
dove (plunged headfirst into water).

Confusing, right? Well, the challenging riddles and comical pictures in this book will help you to recognize and pronounce over seventy common homographs that mix people up every day when they read and speak.

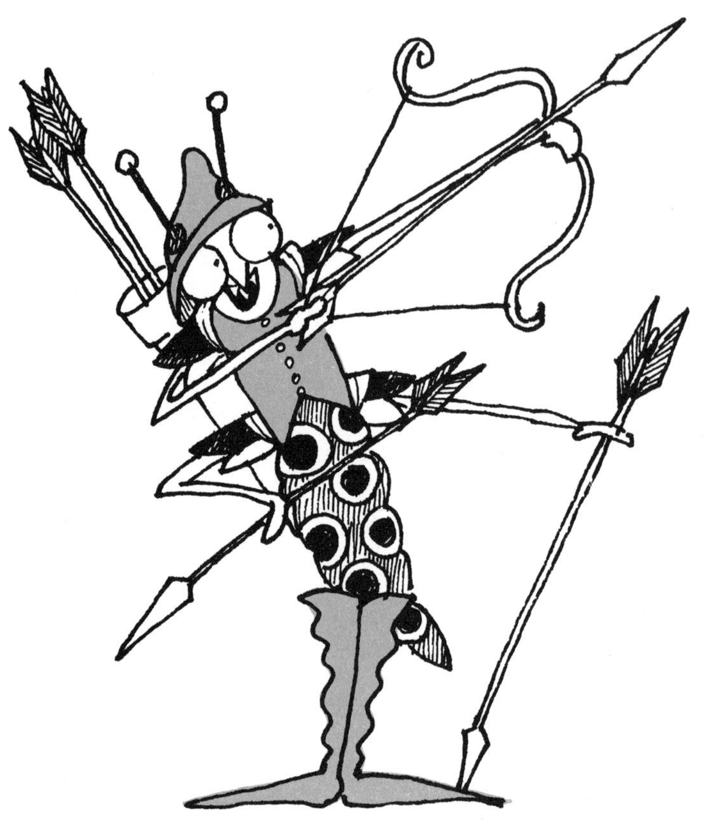

How to Solve These Riddles

Read each riddle sentence. The words in **dark print** are clues to the homographs. Think of how to say the riddle sentence a different way using a pair of homographs instead of the words in dark print. Example:

> *Riddle sentence:* **Bend in respect** to the man with the **weapon that shoots arrows**.
> *Answer:* **Bow** to the man with the **bow**.

Homographs can be bewildering, and some of these riddles are tough. Remember, you have to figure out only one word of every homograph pair. The other word will be spelled exactly the same as the first!

You'll find lots of familiar words, but there will be many new ones, too. So, if you really get stuck, it's OK to peek at the answer words at the bottom of each page. At the end of each chapter, you'll find the full answer sentences and pronunciation guides so you'll know how to say the homographs correctly.

Good luck!

e a u
i o

1

Vowels: Quick Change Artists

Suppose you're reading a story aloud. You come to this sentence:

It's hard to **wind** the wire in this **wind**.

How do you pronounce the two words **wind** and **wind**? You've just bumped into a pair of perplexing homographs.

Sometimes homographs have different vowel sounds. The letters a, e, i, o, or u change sounds from one homograph to the other. When you read the sentence about winding the wire, pronounce the first **wind** with a long i sound (like the i in "Hi!") and the second **wind** with a short i sound (like the i in "win").

The spelling of the homographs always stays the same, of course. Remember, the answer words are at the bottom of each page. The full sentences and pronunciation guides are at the end of each chapter.

One-syllable Words

1. The **fish** sings **low.**

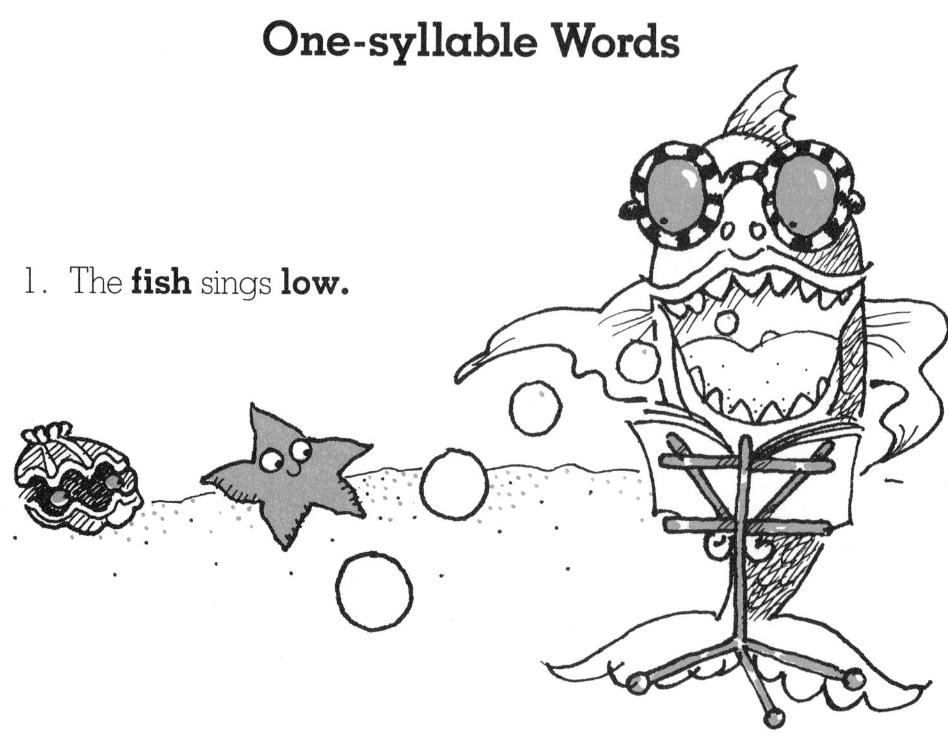

2. **Living** animals **dwell** here.

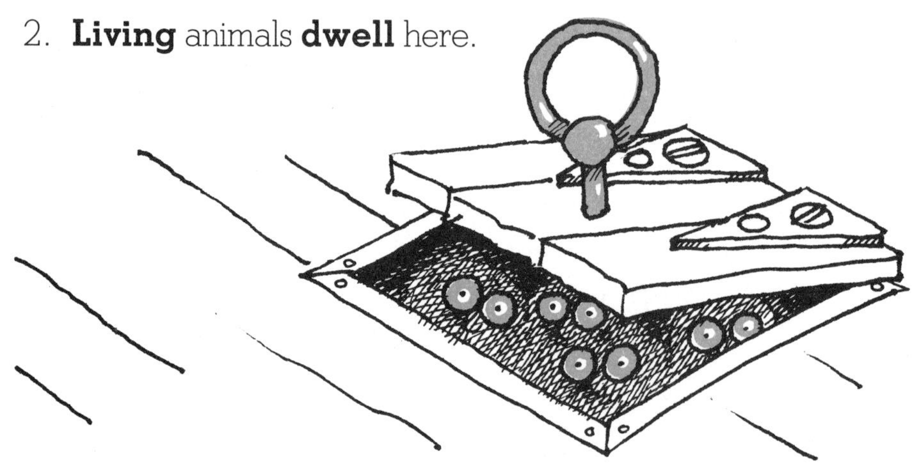

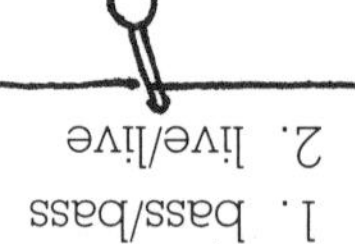

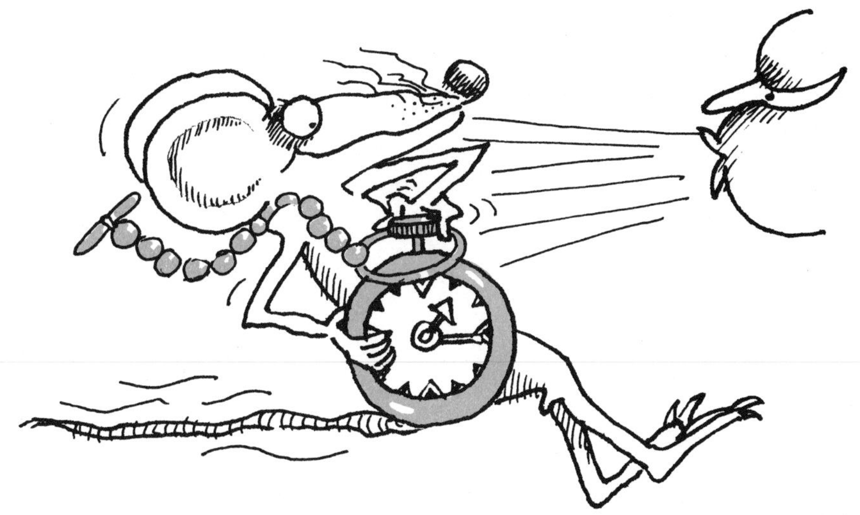

3. In this **strong breeze,** he can't **tighten the spring of** the clock.

4. The girl wearing a **ribbon tied in loops** will **bend in respect.**

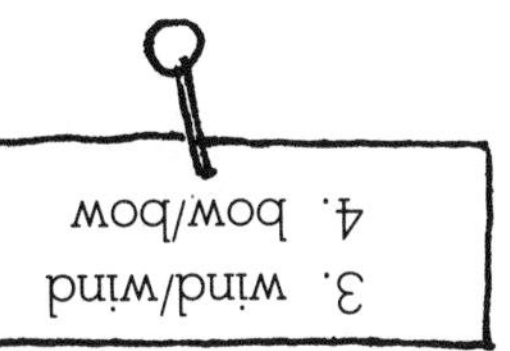

5. **Perform** the **first note on the scale.**

6. The **bird of peace plunged** into the water.

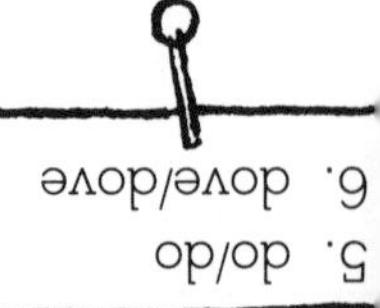

7. My **work** is to teach the story of **thepatient man in the Bible.**

8. They had a **noisy quarrel** about who was going to **paddle the boat.**

7. job/Job
8. row/row

9. **Scatter seeds, female pig!**

In the answers to the next five riddles, two vowels together make one vowel sound.

10. Don't **rip** the picture of the **drop of water in the eye.**

9. sow/sow
10. tear/tear

11. **Guide** me to the **heavy metal.**

12. **Sound out the words** that you **have sounded out** already.

11. lead/lead
12. read/read

13. The nurse **wrapped** the bandage around the **injury.**

14. The zookeeper **performs** tricks with two **female deer.**

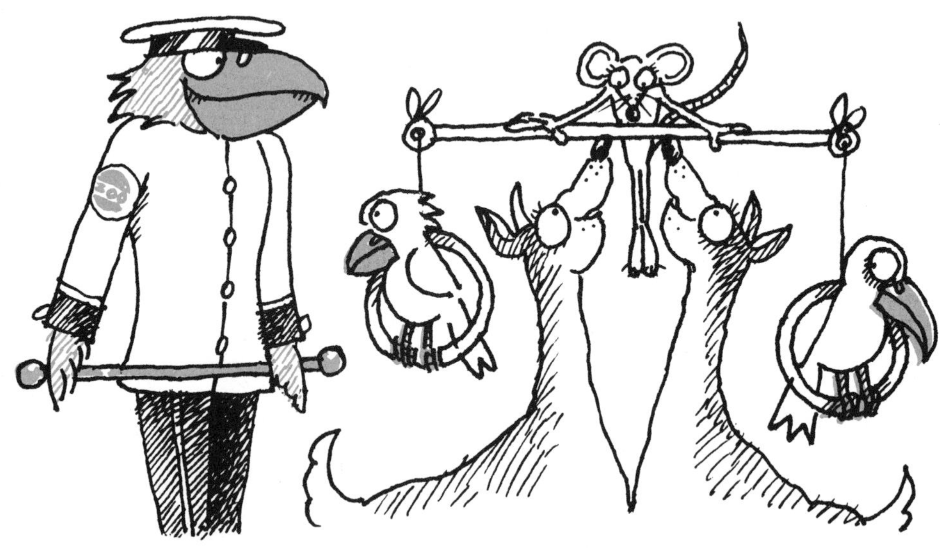

13. wound/wound
14. does/does

Two-syllable Words

In the answers to the following riddles, the sound of one vowel changes in the first syllable.

15. The person **covered with tar** should **delay** awhile.

16. She's the **one who stitches** in the **waste pipe under the street.**

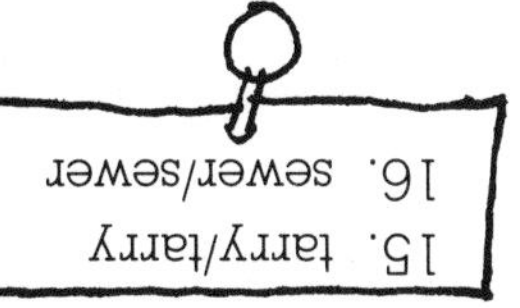

17. They eat **flat green beans** from the **capital of Peru.**

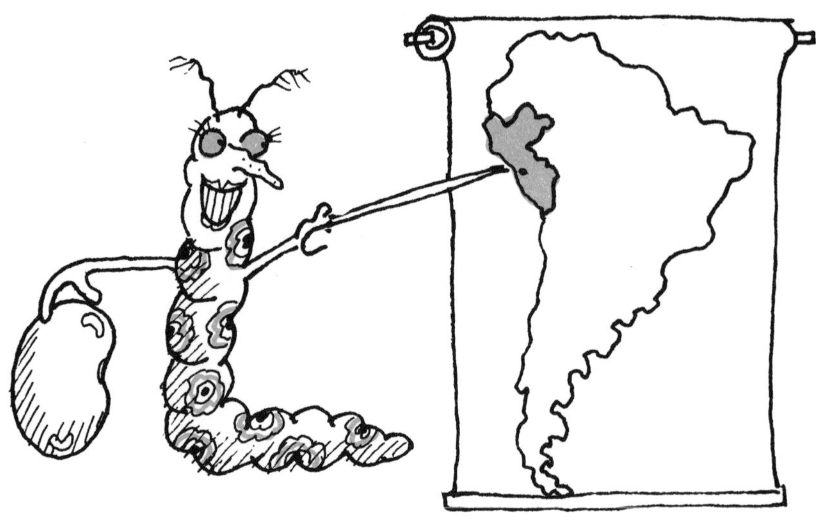

18. That's a **book for beginners** about a **base coat of paint.**

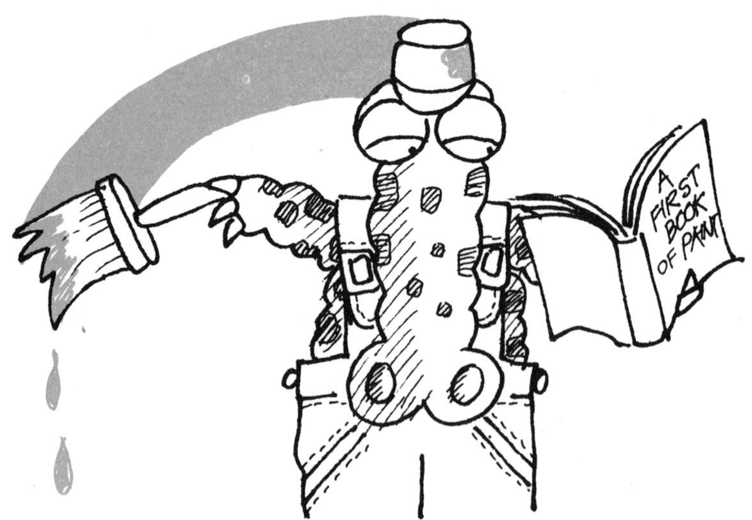

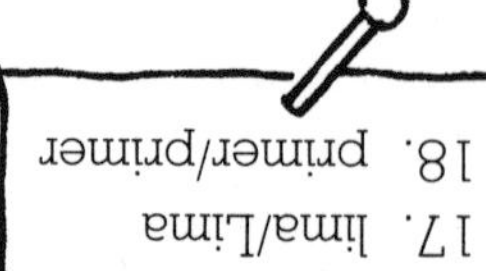

19. I'd like a bottle **from Poland** with **liquid that shines things.**

Three-syllable Words

In the answers to the following riddles, the pronunciation of the third syllable changes from <u>ate</u> to <u>it.</u>

20. When I **receive my diploma**, I'll be a **person who completed school.**

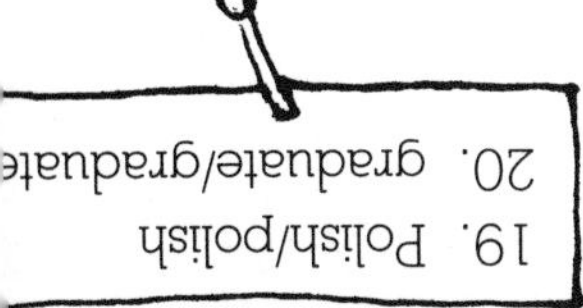

21. Did he **hint at** any **personal or private** details?

22. She'll **be in charge of** the meeting since she has **reasonable** ideas.

21. intimate/intimate
22. moderate/moderate

23. **Divide** the costumes into **different** piles.

24. **Sell** this TV series **to stations** through the **business group**.

1
ANSWERS

How to pronounce the answers to the riddle sentences on pages 14 through 25.

1. The **bass** sings **bass**.
   (bass rhymes with class) (bass rhymes with face)
2. **Live** animals **live** here.
   (live rhymes with five) (live rhymes with give)
3. In this **wind**, he can't **wind** the clock.
   (wind rhymes with grinned) (wind rhymes with kind)
4. The girl wearing a **bow** will **bow**.
   (bow rhymes with go) (bow rhymes with cow)
5. **Do do**. (do rhymes with blew) (do rhymes with blow)
6. The **dove dove** into the water.
   (dove rhymes with glove) (dove rhymes with drove)
7. My **job** is to teach the story of **Job**.
   (job rhymes with bob) (Job rhymes with robe)
8. They had a **row** about who was going to **row**.
   (row rhymes with cow) (row rhymes with go)
9. **Sow, sow**! (sow rhymes with go) (sow rhymes with cow)
10. Don't **tear** the picture of the **tear**.
    (tear rhymes with air) (tear rhymes with ear)
11. **Lead** me to the **lead**.
    (lead rhymes with feed) (lead rhymes with fed)
12. **Read** what you've **read** already.
    (read sounds like reed) (read sounds like red)
13. The nurse **wound** the bandage around the **wound**.
    (wound rhymes with found) (wound rhymes with crooned)

14. The zookeeper **does** tricks with two **does**.
(does rhymes with fuzz) (does rhymes with froze)
15. The **tarry** person should **tarry** awhile.
(tarry rhymes with starry) (tarry rhymes with carry)
16. She's the **sewer** in the **sewer**.
(sewer rhymes with lower) (sewer rhymes with fewer)
17. They eat **lima** beans from **Lima**.
(lima sounds like I'm a...) (Lima sounds like seem a...)
18. That's a **primer** about a **primer**.
(primer rhymes with swimmer) (primer rhymes with climber)
19. I'd like a bottle of **Polish polish**.
(Polish is pronounced pole-ish) (polish rhymes with doll-ish)
20. When I **graduate,** I'll be a **graduate**.
(graduate is pronounced GRAD-u-ate) (graduate is pronounced GRAD-u-it)
21. Did he **intimate** any **intimate** details?
(intimate is pronounced IN-ti-mate) (intimate is pronounced IN-ti-mit)
22. She'll **moderate** the meeting because she has **moderate** ideas.
(moderate is pronounced MOD-er-ate) (moderate is pronounced MOD-er-it)
23. **Separate** the costumes into **separate** piles.
(separate is pronounced SEP-ar-ate) (separate is pronounced SEP-ar-it)
24. **Syndicate** this TV series through the **syndicate**.
(syndicate is pronounced SIN-di-kate) (syndicate is pronounced SIN-di-kit)

2

S or Z? What Should It Be?

In some homograph pairs, the letter s is pronounced as s in one word and as z in the other. Try reading this tricky sentence:

I never stand **close** to the gorilla when I **close** his cage.

In the first close, pronounce the s as s. In the second close, pronounce the s as z.

Answer the following riddles in the same way. If you need to, peek at the answers at the bottom of the page.

25. Don't **mistreat** this pet with **bad treatment**.

26. **Shut** the door fast! Don't let the monster come too **near**.

27. We'll **give a home to** it at the **place where I live**.

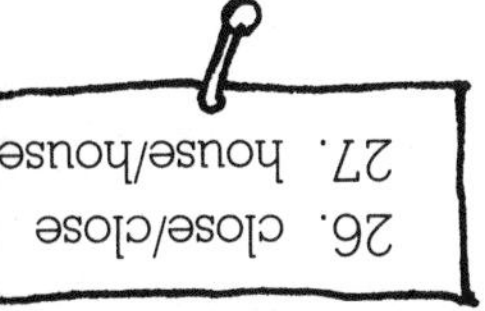

28. **Don't accept garbage**!

29. Can she **do something with** this? Does it have a **purpose**?

28. refuse/refuse
29. use/use

30. **Pardon** me, but I have a **reason** for being late.

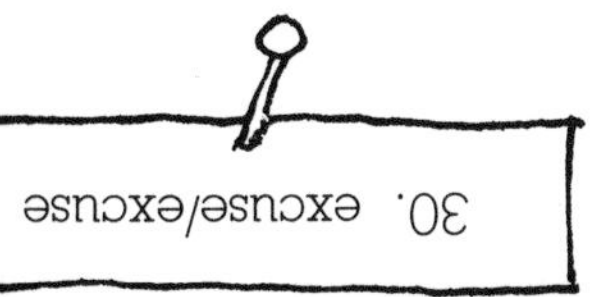

ANSWERS

How to pronounce the answers to the riddle sentences on pages 28 through 31.

25. Don't **abuse** this pet with **abuse**.
    (abuse rhymes with amuse) (abuse rhymes with reduce)
26. **Close** the door fast! Don't let the monster come too **close**.
    (close rhymes with nose) (close rhymes with gross)
27. We'll **house** it at my **house**.
    (house rhymes with browse) (house rhymes with mouse)
28. **Refuse refuse**!
    (refuse rhymes with amuse) (refuse sounds like REF-yoos)
29. Can she **use** this? Does it have a **use**?
    (use rhymes with blues) (use rhymes with juice)
30. **Excuse** me, but I have an **excuse** for being late.
    (excuse rhymes with amuse) (excuse rhymes with reduce)

The Jumping Accent

Here's another riddle sentence with pesky homographs:

> **Remove all faults from** this invention so it will be **faultless**.

The answer is: **Perfect** this invention so it will be **perfect**.

You should put extra stress on "fect" in the first "perfect" and extra stress on "per" in the second "perfect," like this:

> PerFECT this invention so it will be PERfect.

In all the homographs in this chapter, the accent jumps from one syllable to another. In the first homograph in the answer sentence, put extra stress on the second syllable. In the second homograph, put extra stress on the first syllable.

31. Are you **satisfied** with **what is contained** in the package?

32. **Protest** the **competition**.

31. content/content
32. contest/contest

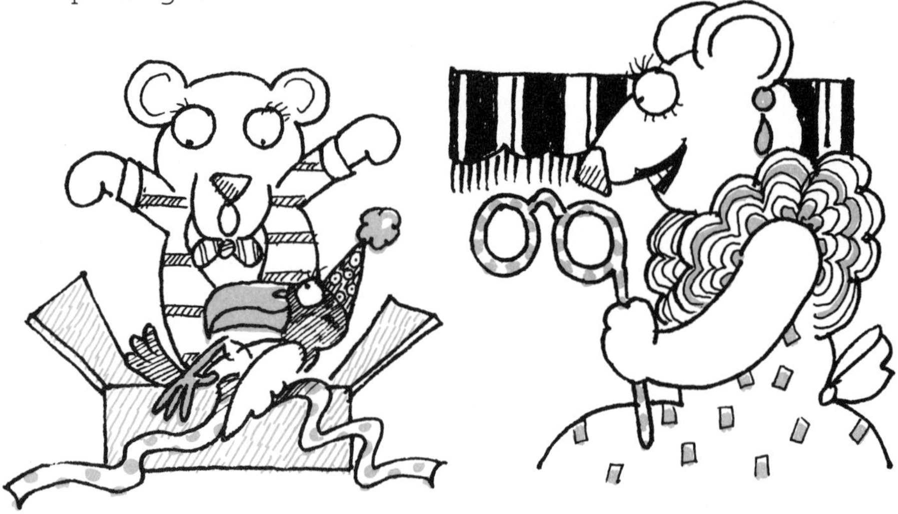

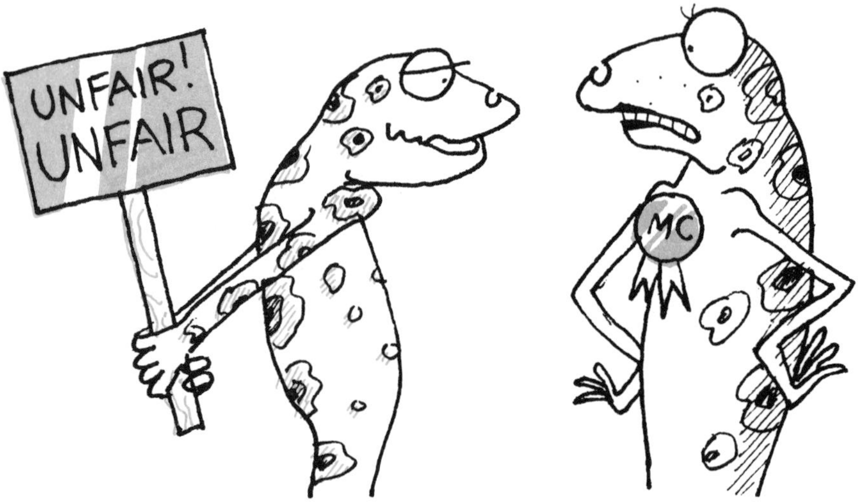

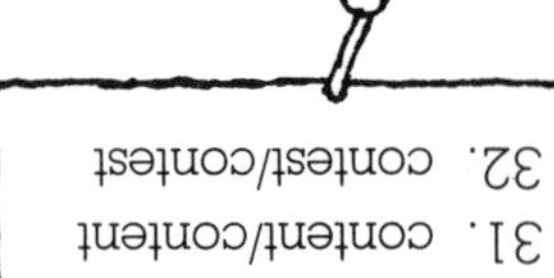

33. I must **change the beliefs of** the **person who adopted new beliefs**.

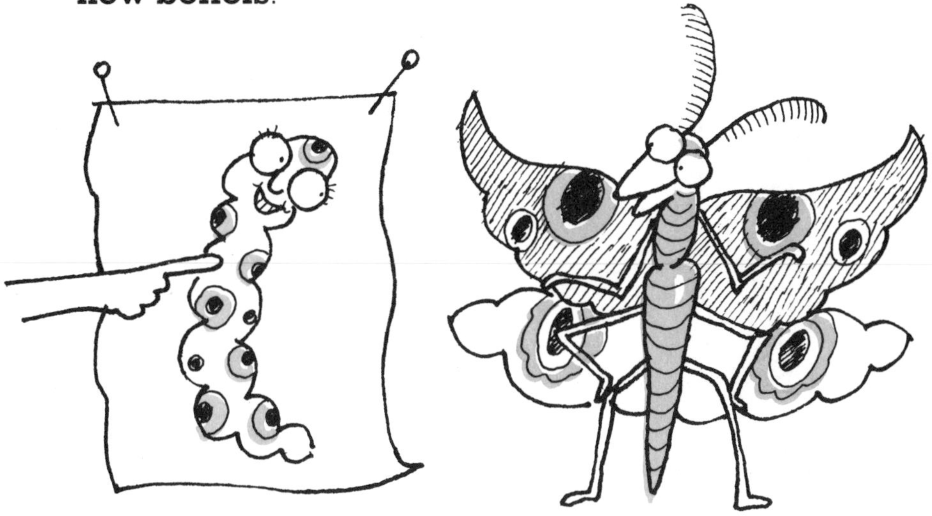

34. The prosecutor tried to **prove the guilt** of the **prisoner**.

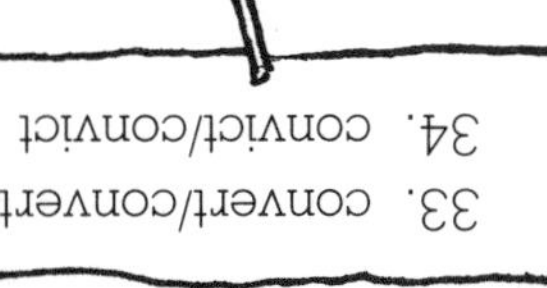

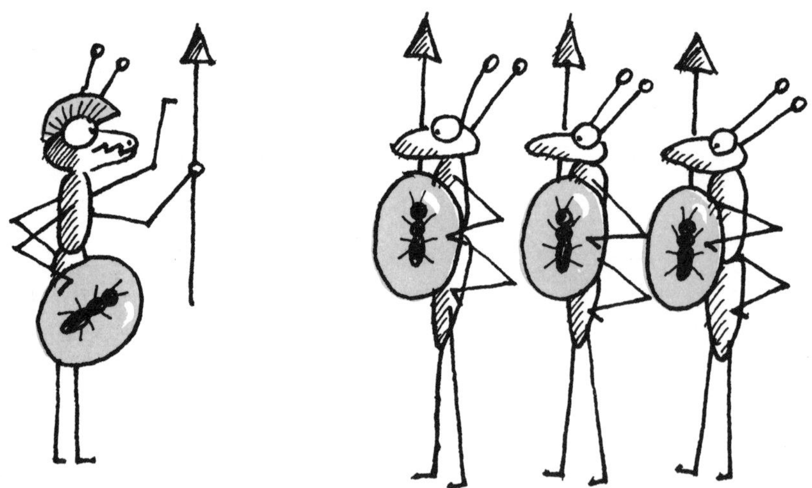

35. You must **fight** against the enemy in **battle**.

36. He'll **talk closely** with the **people who live and work together**.

35. combat/combat
36. commune/commune

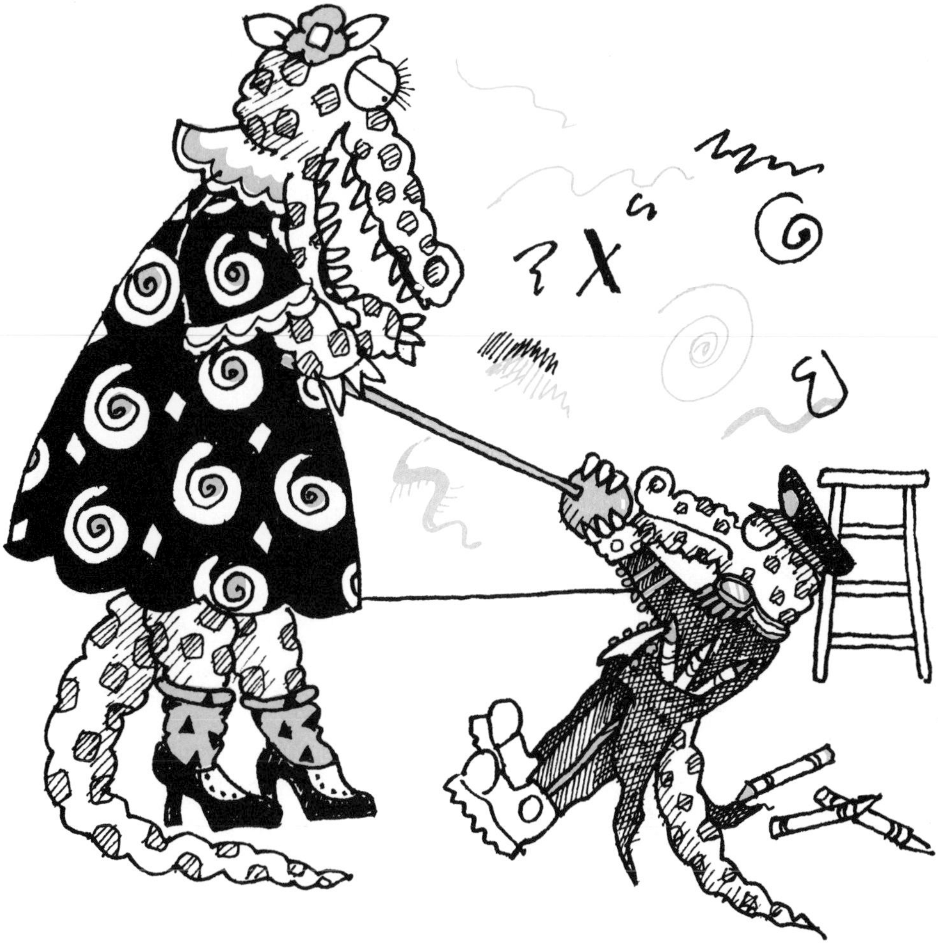

37. You may not **lead** the band if your **behavior** is terrible.

38. **Tightly pack** the garbage into a **firmly packed** package.

37. conduct/conduct
38. compact/compact

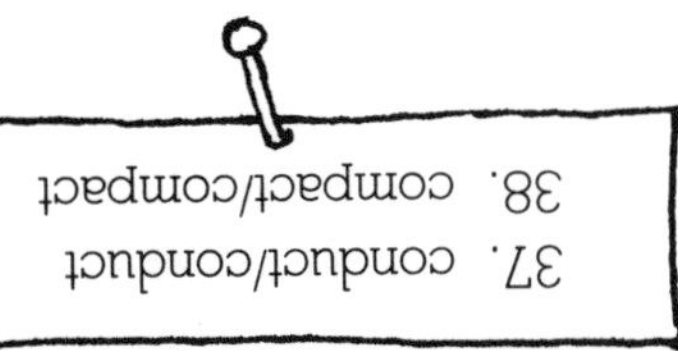

39. **Put together** base and ball to make the **combined word** baseball.

40. **Squeeze** the **cold pad** for my bruise.

39. compound/compound
40. compress/compress

41. **Comfort** me. My television **cabinet** broke.

42. His opinions **differ** from hers in this **struggle**.

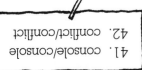

41. console/console
42. conflict/conflict

43. You will **delight and charm** them with your **coming in**.

44. **Accompany** me, **person who accompanies people**.

43. entrance/entrance
44. Escort/Escort

45. Don't **make selfish use of** your **heroic deed**.

46. When they **bring in** foreign goods, it's of great **significance**.

45. exploit/exploit
46. import/import

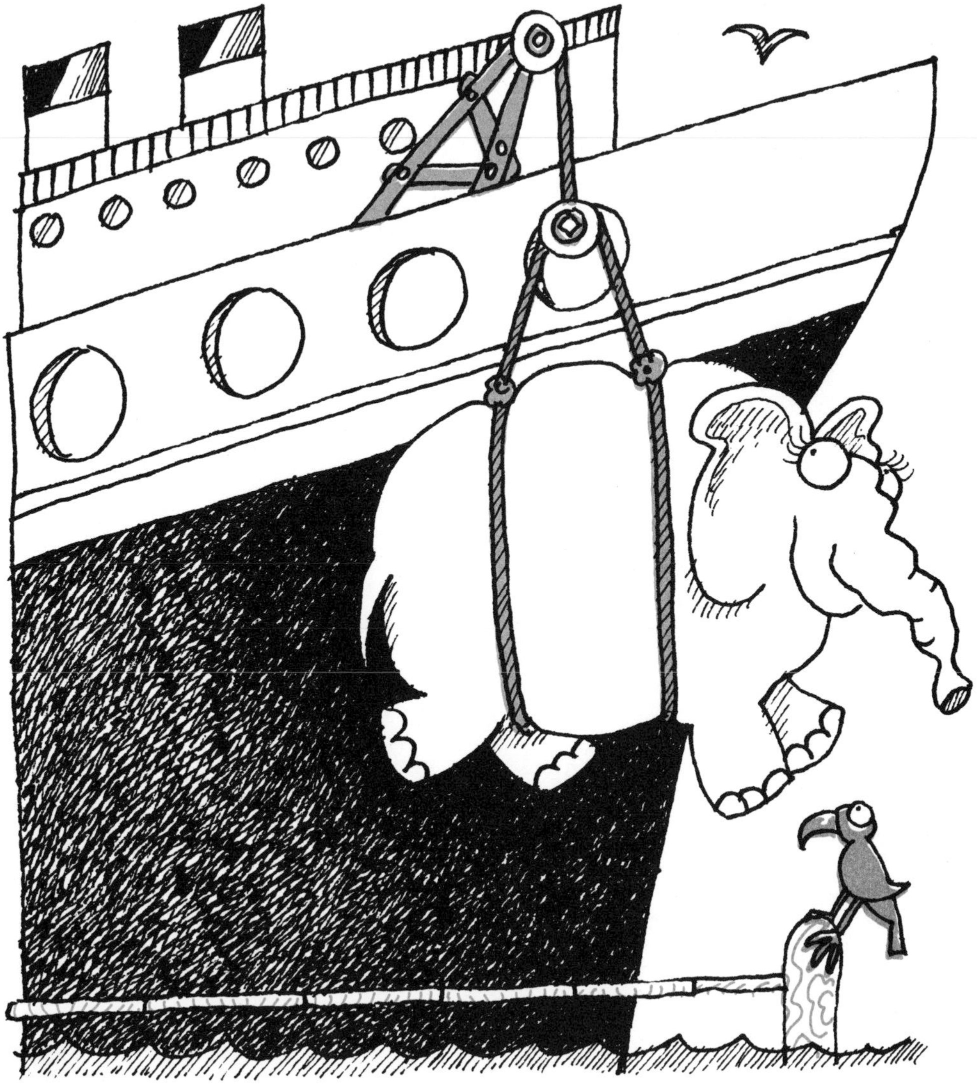

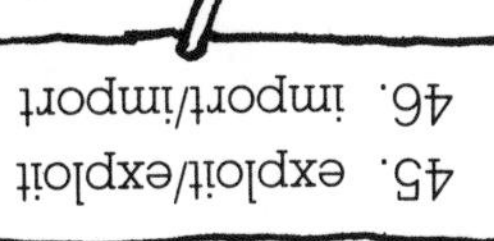

47. It will **enrage** him to smell the **pleasant burning aroma**.

48. You cannot **offend** me with that **rude remark**.

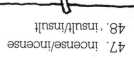

47. incense/incense
48. insult/insult

49. **Confine** the **new doctor in training.**

50. The will that **has no legal force** belongs to the **sick, weak person.**

49. intern/intern
50. invalid/invalid

51. Will you **allow** my **license**?

52. He'll **give** the **gift**.

51. permit/permit
52. present/present

53. If you **move forward**, you'll make **steady improvement**.

54. Set up the screen and **show** a slide of the **plan**.

53. progress/progress
54. project/project

55. I **defy the government,** so call me a **person who resists authority**.

56. She will **make a tape** of this **disc**.

57. I **refuse to take** the **discarded thing**.

58. If I **remove the flower from the pot and replant it in the garden**, it's a **moved plant**.

57. reject/reject
58. transplant/transplar

59. They will **carry** the sailors across the ocean on a navy **ship**.

60. Do you **mistrust** the **suspected person**?

59. transport/transport
60. suspect/suspect

61. I **disapprove** of that **thing**.

62. The **tiny sixty seconds** passed swiftly.

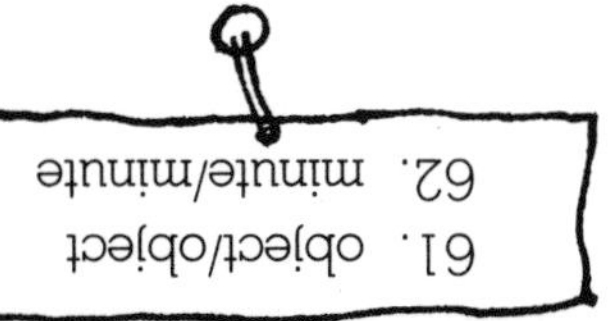

63. That **majestic** person was born in **the eighth month**.

64. Those camels will **abandon** the **sandy land**.

65. The professor **makes us experience** lectures on boring **topics**.

63. august/August
64. desert/desert
65. subjects/subjects

·3·

ANSWERS

How to pronounce the answers to the riddle sentences on pages 34 through 50.

31. Are you **content** with the **content** of the package?
    (content is pronounced conTENT) (content is pronounced CONtent)
32. **Contest** the **contest**.
    (contest is pronounced conTEST) (contest is pronounced CONtest)
33. I must **convert** the **convert**.
    (convert is pronounced conVERT) (convert is pronounced CONvert)
34. The prosecutor tried to **convict** the **convict**.
    (convict is pronounced conVICT) (convict is pronounced CONvict)
35. You must **combat** the enemy in **combat**.
    (combat is pronounced comBAT) (combat is pronounced COMbat)
36. He'll **commune** with the **commune**.
    (commune is pronounced comMUNE) (commune is pronounced COMmune)

37. You may not **conduct** the band if your **conduct** is terrible.
(conduct is pronounced conDUCT) (conduct is pronounced CONduct)
38. **Compact** the garbage into a **compact** package.
(compact is pronounced comPACT) (compact is pronounced COMpact)
39. **Compound** base and ball to make the **compound** baseball.
(compound is pronounced comPOUND) (compound is pronounced COMpound)
40. **Compress** the **compress** for my bruise.
(compress is pronounced comPRESS) (compress is pronounced COMpress)
41. **Console** me. My television **console** broke.
(console is pronounced conSOLE) (console is pronounced CONsole)
42. His opinions **conflict** with hers in this **conflict**.
(conflict is pronounced conFLICT) (conflict is pronounced CONflict)
43. You will **entrance** them with your **entrance**.
(entrance is pronounced enTRANCE) (entrance is pronounced ENtrance)
44. **Escort** me, **Escort**.
(escort is pronounced esCORT) (escort is pronounced EScort)
45. Don't **exploit** your **exploit**.
(exploit is pronounced exPLOIT) (exploit is pronounced EXploit)

46. When they **import** foreign goods, it's of great **import**.
(import is pronounced imPORT) (import is pronounced IMport)
47. It will **incense** him to smell the **incense**.
(incense is pronounced inCENSE) (incense is pronounced INcense)
48. You cannot **insult** me with that **insult**.
(insult is pronounced inSULT) (insult is pronounced INsult)
49. **Intern** the **intern**.
(intern is pronounced inTERN) (intern is pronounced INtern)
50. The will that is **invalid** belongs to the **invalid**.
(invalid is pronounced inVALid) (invalid is pronounced INvalid)
51. Will you **permit** my **permit**?
(permit is pronounced perMIT) (permit is pronounced PERmit)
52. He'll **present** the **present**.
(present is pronounced preSENT) (present is pronounced PRESent)
53. If you **progress**, you'll make **progress**.
(progress is pronounced proGRESS) (progress is pronounced PROGress)
54. Set up the screen and **project** a slide of the **project**.
(project is pronounced proJECT) (project is pronounced PROject)
55. I **rebel**, so call me a **rebel**.
(rebel is pronounced reBEL) (rebel is pronounced REBel)

56. She will **record** this **record**.
(record is pronounced reCORD) (record is pronounced RECord)
57. I **reject** the **reject**.
(reject is pronounced reJECT) (reject is pronounced REject)
58. If I **transplant** the flower, it's a **transplant**.
(transplant is pronounced transPLANT) (transplant is pronounced TRANSplant)
59. They will **transport** the sailors on a navy **transport**.
(transport is pronounced transPORT) (transport is pronounced TRANSport)
60. Do you **suspect** the **suspect**?
(suspect is pronounced susPECT) (suspect is pronounced SUSpect)
61. I **object** to that **object**.
(object is pronounced obJECT) (object is pronounced OBject)
62. The **minute minute** passed swiftly.
(minute is pronounced myNOOT) (minute is pronounced MINit)
63. That **august** person was born in **August**.
(august is pronounced awGUST) (August is pronounced AWgust)
64. Those camels will **desert** the **desert**.
(desert is pronounced diZERT) (desert is pronounced DEZert)
65. The professor **subjects** us to lectures on boring **subjects**.
(subjects is pronounced subJECTS) (subjects is pronounced SUBjects)

Adding Extra Syllables

Sometimes one homograph is pronounced with one syllable and the other homograph is pronounced with two syllables even though the spelling stays the same. For example:

> You keep your socks in a **drawer** (one syllable).
> If you draw pictures, you're a **draw-er** (two syllables).

In this part, pronounce the second homograph in each riddle with one more syllable than the first homograph. The spelling is still the same for both words.

66. We are **favored with fortune** by the **birth of the baby**.

67. He **gained knowledge** from the **scholarly** woman.

68. In his **pointed** cap, he looked **sickly.**

66. blessed/blessed
67. learned/learned
68. peaked/peaked

69. The **thing that slides out of the bureau** was drawn by the **person who draws**.

70. **Go back to** typing my **summary of qualifications for the job.**

69. drawer/drawer
70. resume/resumé

ANSWERS

How to pronounce the answers to the riddle sentences on pages 56 through 57.

66. We are **blessed** by the **blessed** event.
    (blessed sounds like blesst) (blessed sounds like BLESSid)
67. He **learned** from the **learned** woman.
    (learned is pronounced lernd) (learned is pronounced LERnid)
68. In his **peaked** cap, he looked **peaked**.
    (peaked rhymes with peeked) (peaked is pronounced PEEKid)
69. The **drawer** was drawn by the **drawer**.
    (drawer rhymes with roar) (drawer is pronounced DRAWer)
70. **Resume** typing my **resumé**.
    (resume is pronounced reZOOM) (resumé is pronounced REZamay)

·5·

Two Terribly Tricky Homographs

The last two riddles deserve a chapter all their own because they are so challenging. For extra help, use the hints after each riddle. If you get a homograph headache, look at the answers on page 61.

71. This frozen **numeral** is **less able to feel and move** than that one.

Hint: You pronounce the letter b in the first homograph. You don't pronounce that letter in the second homograph.

72. When the waves **knock** against the ship, I can't eat the **foods set out on the table.**

Hints:

1. The final letter in the homographs is t. You pronounce it in the first homograph. You don't pronounce it in the second homograph.
2. The accent jumps from the first syllable in the first homograph to the second syllable in the second homograph.
3. The sound of the vowel e changes.

ANSWERS

How to pronounce the answers to the riddle sentences on pages 59 through 60.

71. This frozen **number** is **number** than that one.
(number sounds like number) (number rhymes with summer)
72. When the waves **buffet** the ship, I can't eat the **buffet**.
(buffet sounds like BUFFit) (buffet sounds like buFAY)

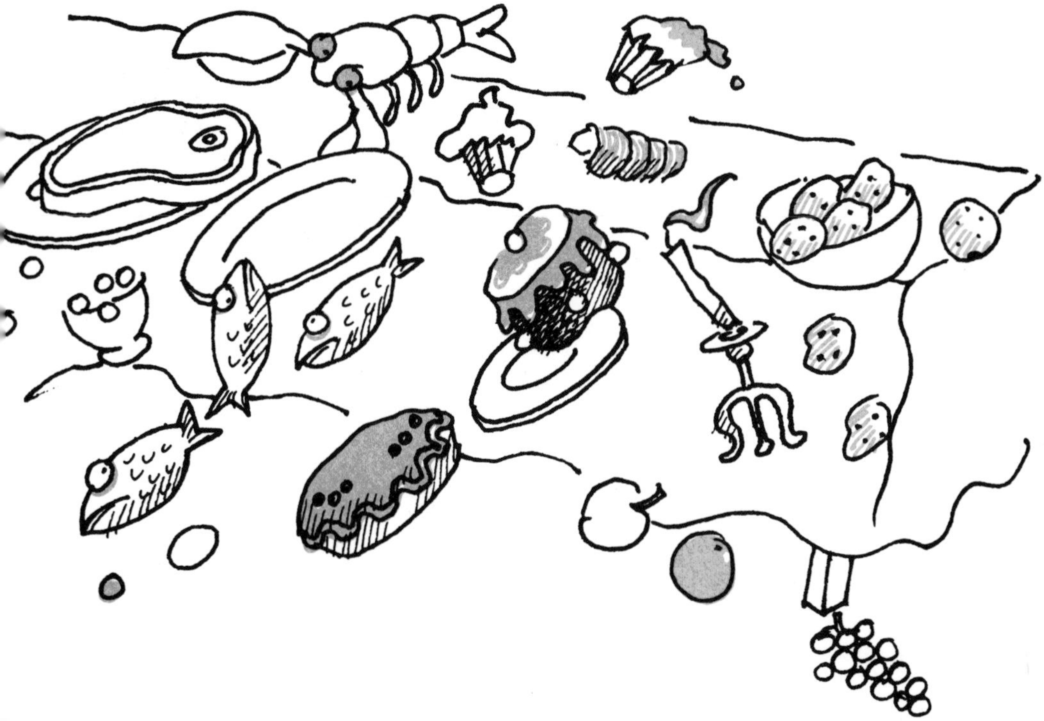

Here is an alphabetical list of the homographs featured in this book.

Homographs	Page Number
permit	44
Polish	23
present	44
primer	22
progress	45
project	45
read	19
rebel	46
record	46
refuse	30
reject	47
resume	57
row	17
separate	25
sewer	21
sow	18
subject	50
suspect	48
syndicate	25
tarry	21
tear	18
transplant	47
transport	48
use	30
wind	15
wound	20